C000064070

THE

Little Book

— OF —

EGYPTIAN
WISDOM

THE
Little Book
— OF —
EGYPTIAN
WISDOM

NAOMI OZANIEC

ELEMENT

Shaftesbury, Dorset ✦ Rockport, Massachusetts
Melbourne, Victoria

© ELEMENT BOOKS LIMITED 1997

Published in Great Britain in 1997 by
ELEMENT BOOKS LIMITED
Shaftesbury, Dorset SP7 9BP

Published in the USA in 1997 by
ELEMENT, INC
PO Box 830, Rockport, MA 01966

Published in Australia in 1997 by
ELEMENT BOOKS LIMITED
and distributed by
Penguin Books Australia Ltd
487 Maroondah Highway, Ringwood, Victoria 3134

Frontispiece: 19th dynasty gold pectoral

Cover illustration: 8th dynasty Egyptian fresco

Designed by
BRIDGEWATER BOOKS

Printed and bound in Singapore by Tien Wah
British Library Cataloguing in Publication data available
Library of Congress Cataloging in Publication data available

ISBN 1 86204 1105

The publishers would like to thank the following for the use of pictures:
e.t. archive, The Bridgeman Art Library

INTRODUCTION

Ancient Egypt has long passed away, yet its wisdom is perennial. We can understand and empathise with words which were written for a very different time and place. It may come as a pleasant surprise to find such simple advice from a people better known for the grandiose and the magnificent.

Egypt was a highly literate civilization with a great regard for the power of the word. A unique genre was developed in this long lived society. The Instructions were written for the education of the scribal class. This important group formed the backbone of Egyptian life.

The Instructions presented a composite picture of the ideal man, the ideal scribe. We should not make the mistake of thinking that such instructions were prepared to regulate the behavior of civil servants and officials of the state. As custodians of knowledge and learning, all scribes were in the service of Thoth, the Lord of Wisdom. In the Instructions we discover the knowledge of the heart which is the timeless place of eternal wisdom. This contemporary selection would surely gladden the heart of any ancient scribe who always believed that the word had the power to endure through time.

Behold, I give you these useful counsels,
For you to ponder in your heart;
Do it and you will be happy,
All evils will be far from you.
Guard against the crime of fraud,
Against words that are not true,
Conquer malice in your self.

extract from *The Instructions of Any*

God prefers him who honors the poor
To him who worships the wealthy.

The Instructions of Amenemope: Chapter 28

Broadcast not your words to others,
Nor join with one who bares his heart.
Better is one whose speech is in his belly
Than he who tells it to cause harm.

The Instructions of Amenemope: Chapter 21

He who knows how to hold his heart has the equivalent of every teaching.

The Ninth Instruction

Don't start a quarrel with a
      hot-mouth man,
Nor needle him with words.
Pause before a foe, bend before an attacker,
Sleep on it before speaking.
A storm that bursts like fire through straw,
Such is the heated man in his hour.
Withdraw from him, leave him alone,
The god knows how to answer him.

The Instructions of Amenemope: Chapter 3

Double the food your mother gave you,
Support her as she supported you;
She had a heavy load in you,
But she did not abandon you,
When you were born after your months,
She was yet yoked to you,
Her breast in your mouth for three years.

extract from *The Instructions of Any*

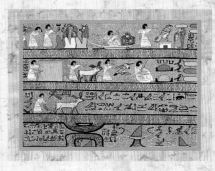

The heart in its smallness sustains its owner.
Many are the small things that are
worthy of respect.
A small benefaction is not hidden
from the god.
A small good news makes the heart live.
The small document has great benefit.
The small falsehood makes trouble for him
who commits it.
The little bee brings the honey.
Few are the great things that are worthy
of admiration.

The Twentieth Instruction

Beware of robbing a wretch,
Of attacking a cripple;
Don't stretch out your hand to touch
    an old man,
Nor open your mouth to an elder.
Don't let yourself be sent on a mischievous
    errand,
Nor be as friends with one who does it.
Don't raise an outcry against one who
    attacks you
Nor answer him yourself.
He who does evil, the shore rejects him,
Its floodwaters carry him away.
The north wind descends to end his hour
It mingles with the thunderstorm,
The storm clouds thunder,
    the crocodiles are vicious,
You heated man, how are you now?

The Instructions of Amenemope: Chapter 2

Do not be greedy, lest your name stink.

The wealth of the generous man is greater
than the wealth of the greedy.

Greed puts strife and combat in the house.

Greed removes shame, mercy and trust
from the heart.

Money is the snare the god has placed on
the earth for the impious man so that he
should worry daily.

He who gives food to the poor, the god
takes to himself in boundless mercy.

The goods of the greedy are ashes driven
by the wind.

The Fifteenth Instruction

The truly silent, who keeps apart,
He is like a tree grown in a meadow.
It greens, it doubles its yield,
It stands in front of its lord.
Its fruit is sweet, its shade is delightful,
Its end comes in the garden.

The Instructions of Amenemope: Chapter 4

What good is one dressed in finery,
If he cheats before the god?
Faience, disguised as gold,
Comes day, it turns to lead.

The Instructions of Amenemope: Chapter 16

Do not let worry flourish lest you become
   distraught.
If the heart worries about its owner it creates
   illness for him.
When worry has arisen, the heart seeks
   death itself.
One day is not like another for him whose
   heart cares.

The Seventeenth Instruction

Keep your tongue free from evil words,
And you will be loved by men.

Put the good remark in your tongue,
While the bad is concealed in your belly.

The Instructions of Amenemope: Chapter 8

Learn about the way of a man
Who undertakes to found his household.
Make a garden, enclose a patch,
In addition to your own plough land;
Set out trees within it,
As shelter about your house.
Fill your hand with all the flowers
That your eye can see;
One has need of all of them
It is a good fortune not to lose them.

extract from *The Instructions of Any*

If a man is observed on a fraudulent errand,
He will not be sent on another occasion.

The Instructions of Amenemope: Chapter 12

Do not set your heart on wealth,
There is no ignoring Fate and Destiny;
Do not let your heart go straying,
Every man comes to his hour.
Do not strain to seek increase,
What you have, let it suffice you.
If riches come to you by theft,
They will not stay the night with you.
Come day they are not in your house,
Their place is seen but they're not there:
Earth opened its mouth, levelled them,
    swallowed them.

The Instructions of Amenemope: Chapter 7

Do the good and you will prosper,
Do not dip your pen to injure a man.

The Instructions of Amenemope: Chapter 15

A quarrelsome man does not rest on
the morrow.
Keep away from a hostile man
Do not let him become your comrade;
Befriend one who is straight and true,
One whose actions you have seen.
If your rightness matches his,
The friendship will be balanced.

extract from *The Instructions of Any*

The pilot who sees from afar,
He will not wreck his boat.

The Instructions of Amenemope: Chapter 26

Do not befriend the heated man,
Nor approach him in conversation.

Swift is the speech of one who is angered,
More than wind over water.
He tears down, he builds up with
    his tongue,
When he makes his hurtful speech.

The Instructions of Amenemope: Chapter 9

The heart of a man is a gift of god,
Beware of neglecting it.

The Instructions of Amenemope: Chapter 24

Do not cheat a man
    through pen upon scroll,
The god abhors it;
Do not bear witness
    with false words,
So as to brush aside another with
    your tongue.
Do not assess a man who has nothing,
And thus falsify your pen.
If you find a large debt against a poor man,
Make it into three parts;
Forgive two, let one stand,
You will find it a path of life.

The Instructions of Amenemope: Chapter 13

Oₙₑ does not discover the heart of a man
in its character if one has not sent him
on a mission.
One does not discover the heart of a wise
man if one has not tested him in
a matter.
One does not discover the heart of an honest
man if one has not sought something
from him.
One does not discover the heart of a
trustworthy man if one has not
consulted him in a deliberation.
One does not discover the heart of a friend
if one has not consulted him in anxiety.
One does not discover the heart of a brother
if one has not begged from him in want.

The Twelfth Instruction

Do not eat bread while another stands by
Without extending your hand to him.
As to food, it is here always,
It is a man who does not last;
One man is rich, another poor,
But food remains for him who shares it.
As to him who was rich last year,
He is a vagabond this year;
Don't be greedy to fill your belly,
Should you come to be in want,
Another may do good to you.

extract from *The Instructions of Any*

Cling to the silent, then you find life,
Your being will prosper upon earth.

The Instructions of Amenemope: Chapter 5

An official is great in his office,
As a well is rich in drawing water.

The Instructions of Amenemope: Chapter 23

A man's belly is wider than a granary,
And full of all kinds of answers;
Choose the good one and say it,
While the bad is shut in your belly.

extract from *The Instructions of Any*

In a town in which you have no family,
    your heart is your family.
A man's good character makes company
    around him.
Do not be close to one in whose heart
    there is hatred.
Better death in want than life in
    shamelessness.
When a wise man is stripped he gives his
    clothes and blesses.

The Twenty-First Instruction

Better is poverty in the hand of the god,
Than bread in the storehouse;
Better is bread with a happy heart,
Than wealth with vexation.

The Instructions of Amenemope: Chapter 6

Do not sever your heart from
your tongue,
That all your strivings may succeed.
You will be weighty before the others,
And secure in the hand of the god.
God hates the falsifier of words,
He greatly abhors the dissembler.

The Instructions of Amenemope: Chapter 10

Do not lie down in fear of tomorrow:
'Comes day, how will tomorrow be?'
Man ignores how tomorrow will be;
God is ever in his perfection,
Man is ever in his failure.

Instructions of Amenemope: Chapter 18

Heart and tongue of the wise man,
  the greatness of their dwelling-place
  is being that of the god.
When heart and tongue are blameless,
  steering results from it.
The work of the god is a joke to the heart
  of a fool.
The life of the fool is a burden to the
  god himself.
The fate and fortune that come, it is the god
  who sends them.

The Twenty-Fourth Instruction

Where there is fraud, success is feeble,
The bad spoils the good.

The Instructions of Amenemope: Chapter 11

Ameasurer who indulges in cheating,
His Eye seals the verdict against him.

The Instructions of Amenemope: Chapter 17

Do not vex your heart.
He will return to praise you soon,
When your hour of rage has
 passed.
If your words please the heart,
The heart tends to accept them:
Choose silence for yourself,
Submit to what he does.

 extract from *The Instructions of Any*

Indeed you should not know the
    plans of god,
And should not weep for tomorrow.

Instructions of Amenemope: Chapter 22

Do not go to court before an official
In order to falsify your words;
Do not vacillate in your answers,
When your witnesses accuse.

The Instructions of Amenemope: Chapter 19

Do not confound a man in the law court,
In order to brush aside one who is right.
Do not incline to the well dressed man,
And rebuff the one in rags.
Don't accept the gift of a powerful man,
And deprive the weak for his sake.

The Instructions of Amenemope:
Chapter 20

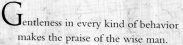

Gentleness in every kind of behavior
   makes the praise of the wise man.
A loud voice causes harm to the parts of the
   body just like an illness.
The counsel that occurs to the fool is as
   weightless as the wind.
Praise is given to the wise man because
   of his calm.
Do not give way often to your tongue to
   advise when you have not been asked.

The Nineteenth Instruction

If one strains to seek perfection,
In a moment he has marred it.
Keep firm your heart, steady your heart,
Do not steer with your tongue;
If a man's tongue is the boat's rudder
The Lord of All is yet its pilot.

The Instructions of Amenemope: Chapter 18

What comes from earth returns
    to it again.
He who thinks of the good is one who
    masters it.
The evil man whose heart loves evil will
find it.

The Twenty-Third Instruction

Look to these thirty chapters,
They inform, they educate;
They are the foremost of books,
They make the ignorant wise.

The Instructions of Amenemope: Chapter 30

Hail to you, great god Lord of justice. I have come to you, my lord, that you may bring me so that I may see your beauty, for I know you and I know your name, and I know the names of the forty-two gods of those who are with you in this hall of Justice.

Lord of Truth is your name. Behold, I have
come to you, I have brought you truth, I
have repelled falsehood for you. I have not
done falsehood against men; I have not
impoverished my associates; I have done no
wrong in the Place of Truth; I have not
learned that which is not; I have done no
evil; I have not daily made labor in excess of
what was due to be done for me; my name
has not reached the offices of those who
control slaves; I have not slandered a
servant to his master; I have not caused pain;
I have not made hungry; I have not made
to weep; I have not killed; I have not
commanded to kill; I have not made
suffering for anyone.

    I am pure, pure, pure.

The Declaration of Innocence

from *The Book of the Dead*

Man is clay and straw,
The god is his builder.

The Instructions of Amenemope: Chapter 25

Do not revile one older than you,
He has seen Re before you;

The Instructions of Amenemope: Chapter 27

Death and the life of tomorrow, we do
    not know their nature.
Today with its livelihood is what the
    wise man asks for.
Neither the impious nor the godly man can
alter the lifetime that was assigned to him.

The Sixteenth Instruction

Beginning of the teaching for life,
The instruction for well-being,
Every rule for relations with elders,
For conduct toward magistrates;
Knowing how to answer to one who speaks
To reply to one who sends a message.
So as to direct him on the paths of life,
To make him prosper upon earth;
To let his heart enter its shrine,
Steering clear of evil;

extract from *The Instructions of Amenemope*

The words men say are one thing,
The deeds of the god are another.
Do not say: 'I have done no wrong,'
And then strain to seek another quarrel;

The Instructions of Amenemope: Chapter 18

ACKNOWLEDGEMENTS

The *Instructions of Amenemope* come from
Miriam Lichtheim: *Ancient Egyptian Literature* Volume
II (The University of California Press, 1976)

The extract from The Book of the Dead is taken from
The Ancient Egyptian Book of the Dead: R.O. Faulkner
(British Museum Publication, 1972)

The extracts from The Instructions of Any come from
Miriam Lichtheim: *Ancient Egyptian Literature* Volume
II (The University of California Press, 1976)

The numbered instructions come from *Ancient
Egyptian Literature* Volume I (The University of
California Press, 1973)